Rhoda

SAM ELLIS'S ISLAND

SAM ELLIS'S ISLAND

by Beatrice Siegel

illustrated by
DyAnne DiSalvo-Ryan

FOUR WINDS PRESS
Macmillan Publishing Company
New York

Collier Macmillan Publishers
London

Macmillan books are available at special discounts
for bulk purchases for sales promotions, premiums,
fund raising, or educational use. Special editions
or book excerpts can also be created to specifica-
tion. For details, contact:

> Special Sales Director
> Macmillan Publishing Company
> 866 Third Avenue
> New York, N.Y. 10022

Macmillan Publishing Company
866 Third Avenue, New York, N.Y. 10022
Collier Macmillan Canada, Inc.

Printed in the United States of America

10   9   8   7   6   5   4   3   2   1

The text of this book is set in 12 pt. ITC Cheltenham Light.
The illustrations are drawn in ink and wash, and
reproduced in black-and-white halftone.

Library of Congress Cataloging-in-Publication Data

Siegel, Beatrice.
   Sam Ellis's island.

   Bibliography: p.
   Includes index.
   Summary: An illustrated history of the tiny island
which at one time was the gateway to the United States
for millions of immigrants.
   1. Ellis Island Immigration Station—History—
Juvenile literature. 2. United States—Emigration and
immigration—History—Juvenile literature. [1. Ellis
Island Immigration Station—History. 2. United States
—Emigration and immigration—History] I. DiSalvo-RyAn,
DyAnne, ill. II. Title.
JV6483.S58 1985   325'.1'0973   85-42799
ISBN 0-02-782720-8

To the memory of my mother and father
Sophie and Samuel

Ellis Island, 1892

ELLIS
ISLAND

A record
of
landfill

Original Island
3.3 Acres

Area Added: 1890

Area Added: 1913

Area Added: 1920

Area Added: 1934

Total Acreage: 27½

Contents

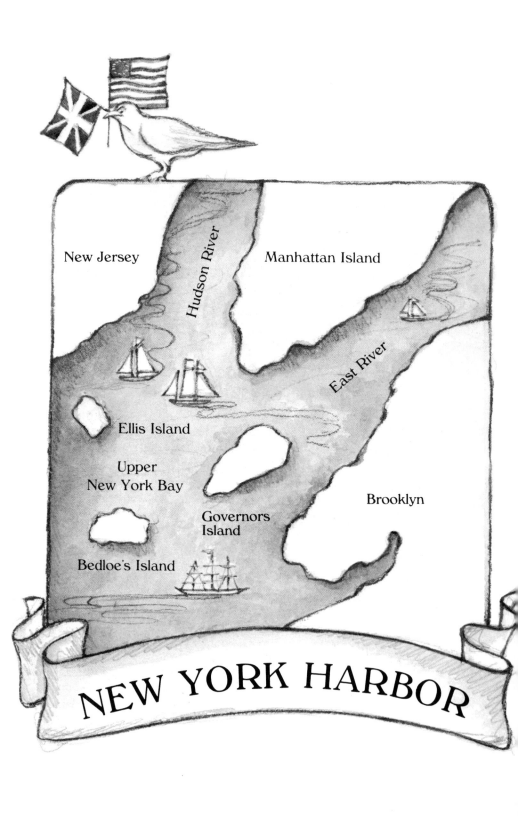

New Jersey

Hudson River

Manhattan Island

East River

Ellis Island

Upper
New York Bay

Governors
Island

Brooklyn

Bedloe's Island

NEW YORK HARBOR

Introduction

No one knows much about Samuel Ellis, though his name designates a strip of land—Ellis Island—known at one time across the world on all continents. Does it matter who Samuel Ellis was? It does if we are interested enough in beginnings, in roots, to ask the question: How did the island get its name?

To find out, we search through slim clues, moving from one piece of evidence to another. We find Sam Ellis alive and prospering at the time of the American Revolution. His property included a tiny island lying peacefully awash by the waters of the Hudson River. But in tracking Sam Ellis, we have found unexpected treasure, the history of the island itself as it changed in shape and size over the years to serve different roles.

In a way the island reflected this country's growth and can be said to be a microcosm of such growth. As we examine its history, not only events come alive but also the great epic movement of people. At one stage, the island was the gateway to the United States. Millions of immigrants came through that gateway. They were an uprooted and fearful mass of people who had left behind all that was familiar—their country, family, and friends. They were sparked by energy and vision, journeying to a strange land to start life anew. Ellis Island became a symbol of their hopes and fears.

What then of Samuel Ellis? How does he fit in? His name hangs over the island like an old sign. It reminds us of bygone days, of change and growth, of a different spirit when a tiny barren piece of land was known simply as Sam Ellis's Island.

A Walker in the Town

In the days when New York was still a British colony, it was nothing more than a seaport town at the tip of Manhattan Island. You could walk from one end to the other in no time at all. And that was what Samuel Ellis often did. He was a familiar sight in his tricorn hat, opened waistcoat, and heavy-soled shoes. Here and there he stopped to greet an acquaintance, to exchange the day's news, and, if lucky, to make a business deal.

Like many of the town's twenty-five thousand inhabitants, Sam Ellis was a merchant. And the big subject of talk was trade, for that was the business of the seaport town—trade. And the sea, wrapped around it on three sides, was its lifeline, connecting it to the countryside and to foreign ports. Wherever Sam Ellis looked, he came up against the sea. On the west side of town, between New York and the colony of New Jersey, flowed the Hudson River (also known as the North River). Across town was the East River. At the face of the seaport both rivers met and flowed out into the Atlantic Ocean, the route to Europe and the families many settlers had left behind.

In back of the seaport stretched a vast continent, the homeland of tribes of Indians. Between them and the settlers existed an uncertain truce. So the first colonists preferred to cling to the coastline and look out over the sea, to watch for the tall, canvas-rigged schooners sailing in from the mother country, England, and from other European ports. The ships would carry cargo, letters from home, newspapers, and people. The town rejoiced at the steady flow of newcomers. They brought with them the latest news, their many skills, and up-to-date styles from the old country.

Amid these hectic goings-on, Sam Ellis was widely known in the town as a dealer in wholesale fish. He advertised in the local newspaper:

SAMUEL ELLIS HAS FOR SALE FAT SHAD, LEAN SHAD AND FAT HERRING, OPPOSITE THE BEAR MARKET: AT THE NORTH RIVER.

Sam dealt not only in fish but also in general merchandise. When schooners sailed in from England, he would poke his head into the cargo and put in his bid for hardware, paint, paper, or twine—whatever he could profitably buy and sell.

In search of business, he wandered along the waterfront into markets and warehouses. Sometimes he would drop in on Smith Ramadge, a dry-goods importer on Queen Street, from whom he had recently bought a parcel of land. Or he would stop off for a drink at a crowded tavern along the dock, where he would pass the time listening to burly seamen tell tales about exotic faraway ports. Walking along the narrow streets, he would pass the shops of the skilled artisans: the candlemaker, the clockmaker, and the silversmith. And when he reached the Broad Way, a wide, tree-lined street, he broke into long strides, always careful to

1763

dodge the wheels of horse-drawn carriages and oxcarts. For the Broad Way led from Fort George, at the southern tip of the island, northwest to his home.

Home for Sam Ellis was One Greenwich Street. There he lived with his wife, Mary, and his children. It was not the elegant section of town. The wealthy people had built homes to the south, near the fort in St. George's Square. Commerce was centered along the East River, and the west side was a neighborhood of modest homes and businesses. It was upgraded, however, by scholars and students attending nearby King's College and the wealthy who worshiped at St. Paul's Parish Church on Vesey Street. Everywhere Sam could see signs of growing commercial development. The Bear Market near his home was expanding. Docks and wharves were being added along the Hudson. At the same time, the soft green hills were being leveled; swamps and ponds, filled in to create flat, usable land.

Everything was new. Greenwich Street, built on landfill along the Hudson River, had made its appearance only ten years before, in 1763. It became the fastest route between the seaport and the little village called Greenwich to the north.

Not only the land but the Hudson as well changed with the increasing commerce. From his home Sam Ellis could look down to the busy river traffic. Boats laden with furs and timber sailed down the river into the harbor. Fast-moving Indian canoes darted among sloops and barges while oystermen guided light skiffs from New Jersey to New York to deliver their catch of fat, juicy oysters. Pushing back and forth on its regular run was the Cortlandt Street ferry connecting New York to Paulus Hook in New Jersey.

Sam Ellis could see signs of the future. Anyone involved in business could judge the vitality of the town, that it was bursting with energy and extending north into the wilderness.

And Sam was eager to prosper along with it. In April 1775, he undertook from Trinity Church a ninety-nine-year lease on fourteen lots of land. They adjoined each other on Greenwich Street near Barclay along the waterfront. Included in the transaction were rights to houses, lofts, soil, and grounds.

At about the same time, Sam Ellis came into possession of a tiny island close to the Jersey shore. It was nothing much, a flat, treeless, desolate bit of land 3.3 acres in size that no one seemed to care about. The island lay so low in the water that it almost disappeared when the sea rolled in at high tide.

Nevertheless, he thought the island could prove valuable. He could expand his fisheries and cast nets for shad and other species of herring that ran in the spring. He could also use it for storage of tools and boats. Sam knew, too, that in the shallow, muddy waters around the island were rich beds of oysters and other shellfish.

In fact, this strip of land was one of the three small Oyster Islands. They grew out of the oyster banks along the Jersey shore in what is called Upper New York Bay. One of the others, named Bedloe's Island, was larger and had fertile soil and fresh springwater. The third, a rock jutting out of the water at low tide, had no name at all. The three islands, buffeted by the eternal ebb and flow of the Hudson, seemed to be relics of a long-ago age.

That was the way Sam Ellis sometimes viewed his island when he stood on the New York shore, shaded his eyes against the glaring sun and looked out across the river. It had a new name now, having quickly become known as Sam Ellis's Island. But in the steady sparkle of the sun on the river, Sam could reflect that one hundred and fifty years earlier the island had belonged to the Indian people.

Gulls and Pirates

The Indians had called it Kioshk or Gull Island. It was only a barren sandbar in a huge landscape of sea and forests. In summers they dug around the island for oysters and clams. But in general they left it in its natural state, a preserve for wildlife. Most of the time flocks of gulls made the island their feeding ground, hovering overhead, breaking the silence with their raucous screeches. Or the gulls idled wing to wing along the island's edge, grabbing up hard-shelled oysters in their beaks and flying off in a noisy flutter with their prey.

The explorer Henry Hudson noticed the magnificence of the land when he sailed his ship, the *Half Moon*, into New York Bay in 1609. Hudson was searching for the gold, jewels, and spices of the Indies. Instead he had penetrated the coastal waters of another world. "This is a very good land to fall in with, and a pleasant land to see," his assistant navigator wrote in his journal. The crew of twenty hung from the riggings and over the railings to stare at the friendly but strange people who waved to them. All the way up the river that would bear his name, Hudson remarked on the fields of Indian corn, majestic mountains, and dense woodlands.

Still, like explorers before and after him, Henry Hudson had come with trade in mind. So he measured the land's wealth as if he were a surveyor. Forests teeming with animals meant furs for the courts of Europe; tall stands of trees meant timber for ships and homes. He calculated the profits in trees laden with fruit and nuts, and in rivers rich with fish.

Though Henry Hudson was English born, he sailed in the service of Holland. Following his explorations, a large commercial organization, the Dutch West India Company, sent settlers to set up a trading post and to deal in furs with the Indians.

By 1626 the Dutch had bought Manhattan Island from the Manhatta Indians and founded a seaport town. They called it New Netherland. Clinging to the edge of the continent, they began to transform the wilderness into towns and farms that reminded them of home. They built a colony close to their fort, Fort Amsterdam, and constructed neat, gabled houses, tulip gardens, windmills, and a church. On the slopes were pastured goats and sheep. West of the fort they erected a gallows as a warning to lawbreakers.

The Dutch worked hard, and trade was so good that they needed more people. By 1629 the Dutch government had introduced the patroon system. It granted vast tracts of land in the "new world" to aristocrats and wealthy merchants on condition that they send over colonists. In this way Gull Island came into the hands of its first private owner.

Had Samuel Ellis lived a century and a half earlier, he would certainly have seen eye to eye with the Dutch aristocrat Michael De Paauw. De Paauw won a grant of land across from Manhattan in New Jersey. He also gained ownership of the offshore islands. In the tradition of feudal landlords, De Paauw named his estate Pavonia, meaning peacock. And then he renamed Gull Island. He called it Oyster Island, which made good sense as a form of advertising. De Paauw, a merchant at heart, realized that oysters and other shellfish could be sold at a profit. Taverns and markets were ready-made customers. And when cured, the shellfish could be shipped to Europe and the West Indies.

De Paauw failed to send over the required fifty colonists, and he had to give up his land. But it remained Pavonia to pioneer settlers who built scattered farms in the wilderness. Oyster Island, however, changed names in the course of events. For the seaport did not stand still.

11

Without firing a shot, the British took over Manhattan Island from the Dutch in 1664. New Amsterdam became New York after the English Duke of York, who was in charge of the region. Fort Amsterdam became Fort George to honor King George of England. And the population of fifteen hundred steadily increased with the continuous influx of newcomers. Most were English, but others came from all over Western Europe. By 1690 eighteen different languages could be heard in the seaport. Its population now included Germans, Scotch-Irish, Scandinavians, French Huguenots, Belgian Walloons, and Portuguese and Spanish Jews. Each religious group established its own church, for the Dutch had laid the cornerstone for religious freedom in the colony.

Not everyone enjoyed freedom. Black people, brought in chains from Africa and the West Indies as early as 1619, were bought and sold on the Wall Street slave market. Prisoners of war and indentured servants were also brought in. A local newspaper announced a sale aboard the ship *Commerce,* just arrived from Scotland, of "a number of Weavers, Taylors, Blacksmiths, Nailors, Shoemakers, Butchers, Hatters—from 14 to 35 years of age." Indentured servants usually won their freedom after seven years in bondage.

Within the lively seaport a complex society was being established. Slaves, indentured servants, merchants, and aristocrats were contributing to the creation of a booming commercial center.

To get away from the noisy, bustling town, boatloads of colonists rowed over to Oyster Island for picnics and oyster roasts. Young lovers used the island as a meeting place.

In the following years the island went through a series of different owners, starting with New York's Governor Andros, who presented it as a gift to Captain William Dyre.

Dyre had been collector of customs and later became mayor of New York. It was Dyre's Island until he sold it to the Lloyd family, who in turn sold it in 1691. At about the same time, New York won a jurisdictional fight with New Jersey over all the Oyster Islands. For the next eighty years, the bit of land was called Bucking Island, although its ownership remains a mystery.

In 1757 the seaport faced a crisis. Town officials needed an isolated spot for a pesthouse, a shelter for people with contagious diseases. They considered Bucking Island but could not find a freshwater spring. Bedloe's Island was more suitable and it became the town's first quarantine center.

Growth was taking place on land and on sea. The widely separated settlements were growing into colonies, connected to each other socially and economically. Colonial ships carried freight to Europe and other foreign ports.

The sea meant high adventure to young men. It took daring to sail wooden vessels over the ocean. For many it offered escape from back-breaking farm work. Drawing them was the lure of foreign ports, and possible wealth. And it was true that a few seamen did grow rich as merchants.

But the sea was dangerous. Privateers and pirates roamed freely, seizing and plundering ships and killing crews. Privateering was a form of warfare, encouraged by governments expecting to share in the plunder of enemy ships and in the division of the spoils. The renowned English "seadogs," Francis Drake and Walter Raleigh, were knighted for their exploits.

Privateering, however, often turned into piracy. Pirates seized both enemy and friendly ships, and divided the spoils between captain and crew. Such robbery on the high seas became costly both to governments and commerce, and countries began to protect their shipping with the use of navies.

The English government signaled a change in policy when it captured, tried, and hanged the popular pirate Captain Kidd. Though piracy began to wane, attacks continued to threaten shipping. One such act destroyed the calm of Oyster Island.

It happened in 1765, when two seamen sailing from New York to the West Indies with a boatload of passengers seized the vessel near the ship's destination. They killed the other crew members and all the passengers except a young boy. After a drunken spree to celebrate the event, the ship came in sight of St. Thomas Island. The youngster was ordered to row the two seamen to port. He did so, and when he could escape he notified the police of the crime. One of the two seamen ran off to St. Eustatius Island where he was arrested and tortured to death. The other, named Anderson, was arrested and sent back to New York to stand trial. He was sentenced to death by hanging. The site selected for the hanging was Oyster—or Bucking—Island. A gallows was quickly erected.

The hanging became a gala event, a day for picnics and celebrations. Boats crowded with grownups and children thronged around the island to watch an execution at the gallows.

Afterward, the island was renamed. It became Gibbet or Anderson Island.

A few years later, in 1769, another pirate, named Andrews, was hung in irons near the Washington Market before he was removed to Gibbet Island and put to death. Intermittently criminals were ferried over to the island and executed.

By the time Samuel Ellis became the island's owner in the 1770s, it had gone through countless name changes: Kioshk, Oyster, Dyre, Bucking, Gibbet, Anderson. And it had served different functions, from a feeding ground for gulls to a hanging ground for pirates.

But for Sam Ellis it offered a peaceful future. He rowed back and forth across the Hudson, happily watching his fishing nets fill with shad in the fast-running river. His pleasure was brief. News reached him of a military skirmish up north in Massachusetts. Shots had been fired between colonists and British redcoats at Lexington and Concord in April 1775, and he knew it meant war.

"New York was aflame with excitement," wrote historian Martha Lamb. "The news traveled with the speed of a whirlwind, and the whole city . . . seemed to have risen in resentment. Men hurried to and fro, women were met weeping on the sidewalks, the churches were deserted in the great feverish impulse to learn the miserable truth. . . ."

The thirteen colonies from Maine to Georgia were put on alert. Those gunshots announced the beginning of the American Revolution and the fight for independence from Great Britain. One year later, when the Declaration of Independence was signed on July 4, 1776, Sam Ellis already knew which side he was on.

King George and George Washington

George Washington was not Sam's hero. Nor for that matter was Paul Revere, Samuel Adams, or Thomas Paine. These men were arousing the countryside to take up arms against Great Britain and fight for freedom. They were called rebels or patriots. Sam Ellis, on the other hand, was a Tory or loyalist. He joined those who wanted to retain their ties to Great Britain, swearing fealty to King George III.

Sam barely shrugged at the issue of taxation without representation. He did not like all those taxes imposed by the British in the 1760s—the Stamp Act, the Sugar Act, and many others. But neither did he join the protests organized by the Sons of Liberty and Daughters of Liberty. These militant rebels marched down the streets, holding aloft effigies of pro-British government leaders. They built gallows, hanged the effigies, and set them on fire.

No doubt Sam stayed at home behind locked doors when rebels massed at the southern tip of town in the Bowling

Green and toppled the statue of King George off its pedestal. He could hear their gleeful shouts of victory when they hauled away the loot. The four thousand pounds of lead would be used for bullets, they said.

Such lawlessness frightened Sam Ellis and other Tories. Uprisings against King George could only make trouble and interfere with business. Where would it end?

In the first year of the Revolutionary War, fighting was

concentrated in New England. After the defeat of the British in Boston, George Washington knew that the city of New York would be the next serious line of defense. He ordered the rebel armies to head south. In a panorama of movement, regiments on horse and on foot moved into New York. They looked like patches of vivid fabric pieced together, each colonial regiment in a different color and style of uniform—the New Jersey soldiers in blue, the Maryland

men in bright scarlet, the Pennsylvanians in green, and those from Connecticut in brown.

By April 1776, George Washington had shifted his headquarters to New York to oversee the defense of the city. The rebels were confident. They set up Committees of Safety. They mounted batteries on every slope, barricaded the streets, built redoubts, or strongholds, along the waterfront, and forbade the civilian population to have any contact with the British army or fleet. To make bullets, they ripped lead from roofs and windowsills. And to protect the Hudson River from invasion, they erected fortifications at Red Hook and Paulus Hook.

Everyone was girding for war, the only topic of talk. "We all live here like nuns shut up in a nunnery. No society with the town . . . nor can we leave and return without permission," wrote one soldier. "A general ruin seems to have overspread the whole face of the earth . . . ," wrote another.

As the spring of 1776 wore on, General Washington foresaw a "bloody summer." The British had landed a formidable army on Staten Island. Their huge fleet was sailing into the harbor. This show of British strength spread both fear and determination among the rebels. The Tories, Sam Ellis among them, carefully went about their business, keeping their political persuasions to themselves, for the townspeople and militia were alert to the danger of Tory neighbors. Many took personal vengeance against these enemies within the city. They rode the Tories through the streets on rails and tore the clothes from their backs, among them Queen, the apothecary, and Leslie, the barber. They tarred and feathered a shoemaker named Tweedy.

They uncovered a supposed Tory conspiracy to assassinate George Washington and other officers, and a soldier

22

was accused of the crime and hanged. It marked the first military execution of the war.

George Washington and his armies came face to face with the British in the battle of Brooklyn Heights in August 1776. Against the well-organized, well-armed British, Washington's rebel army did not stand a chance. They lost that battle. It looked as if Washington and his nine thousand men would be captured, and the war would be over in one blow. But Washington did not give up. He ordered his men to retreat. And he called on every ship and raft that could stay afloat to carry his defeated army across the East River back into Manhattan.

From night until morning General Washington rode among his men directing the evacuation. He saw every soldier safely into a boat before he himself finally embarked. In the dead of night an armada of rafts and skiffs sailed across the East River. In the morning a heavy mist shrouded their movements. The armies landed in Manhattan. Despite an order to hold the port of New York, Washington knew it could not be done. Most of his men made their way north through the rocky heights of Harlem into White Plains. Others in the rebel army tried to hold the British off, fighting a skirmish at Kips Bay on the East River. They too then retreated north.

The defeat of Washington and his army in Brooklyn Heights brought panic to New York City. Three-quarters of the population supported the rebels. They hastily threw together a few possessions and followed the army out of the city. They filled wagons and carriages. They rode on horseback. Thousands—men, women, and children—fled the city on foot. Homes were deserted, businesses dismantled. Families were torn apart, children against parents, sisters and brothers taking different sides in the war.

In the seaport of New York Sam Ellis joined other Tories in the wild cheering and celebrations of victory. They saw British troops, protected by heavy cannon fire, land on September 15, 1776. For seven years of the Revolutionary War, New York City was occupied by the British. It had become a Tory stronghold.

A week after the British occupation, a fire of unknown origin (though blamed on the rebels) broke out on the lower Broad Way. Sam Ellis watched the roaring flames sweep northward and west to the river, destroying a third of the city. He saw Trinity, the church of England, swallowed up in flames. About five hundred small homes, most of them made of wood, crackled and crumbled. St. Paul's Chapel on Vesey Street, where Sam and his family worshiped, was saved by a hastily organized bucket brigade that doused the flames from the roof. King's College was spared.

Maybe the Tories needed a scapegoat. On the following day, September 22, they executed the rebel soldier Nathan Hale as a spy.

Thus, amid fire and execution, the British began their occupation of New York. Through it all Sam Ellis stayed at home at One Greenwich Street. He was one of about five thousand who chose to remain with the British. They represented all ranks: wealthy landowners and business people; small merchants like Sam Ellis; and poor artisans and laborers.

Settled in with his cronies, Sam did not feel lonely. The pro-British Anglican clergy remained in New York, among them Benjamin Moore, assistant rector of St. Paul's. Nearby was his friend Balthazar Creamer, who would later own land near his on Greenwich Street. New York, now a Tory haven, was filling up with loyalist families fleeing from the rebel armies.

In the turmoil of changing sides, all loyalist property was protected. Rebel homes and land were confiscated, taken over by the British to house their army. Deserted churches, warehouses, schools, and cargo ships were used as prisons for rebel soldiers, twelve thousand of whom would perish from starvation, thirst, and the neglect of their wounds before the war came to an end.

A month after the British occupation, in October 1776, Sam Ellis was one of 948 residents who signed a petition expressing support of the commanders of the British army and fleet. He also added his signature to a petition that expressed loyalty to England and its king. But while Sam Ellis expressed support for the British, neither he nor his family played active roles on committees formed to safeguard the city.

Even for those who supported the crown, life was not easy in a seaport under military occupation. In 1778 another fire of unknown origin broke out. Though less destructive than the fire of 1776, it added to the bleak and charred look of the city. Rubbish piled up on neglected streets. Buildings were collapsing. Rents and prices of food skyrocketed, making many rich as a result of the war. Schools were closed. (King's College, closed for the duration, would reopen as Columbia College after the war.)

The army issued strict regulations for maintaining order. To keep the city clean, a ruling made it a crime to throw garbage out of windows. Passes were required to leave or enter the city. Rules specifically restricted use of the waterways. Special licenses were needed to fish, and fees were charged to cart fish on ferries. The size of privately owned boats was limited. In addition, no one could use the wharves after dark.

The Hudson River was a gateway to the north. If the British could control the river straight up to Canada, they would cut George Washington and his troops off from New England and bring the war to an end. British gunboats patrolled the river, also on the alert for spies who might blow up their ships. Part of the fleet was stationed at Paulus Hook, near Sam Ellis's Island.

To get over to his island, Sam Ellis needed a special pass permitting him to use a small boat. He needed a pass to fish, and he could cross the river only between sunrise and sundown.

Whatever his political beliefs, Sam Ellis was first and foremost a merchant. Any restrictions made operating his fisheries difficult. His island seemed far away and useless. Not only had the British curtailed use of the Hudson, they had also taken over the Bear Market down the street. They turned it into a storage depot for hay, grain, and straw. Often, a troop of cavalry was stationed there.

Still, Sam found the years profitable. The city remained quiet and prosperous while the war was being fought across the river and up north. He made money in the soaring prices of produce, finding new customers in the British army and the thousands of loyalists who had settled in the town. And while the blast of cannons sounded in the distance, he took care of his property.

He paved a street near the fourteen lots he had leased from Trinity Church. Along his property he built a slip, an opening to the river. He also put up a new building on Greenwich Street near the Hay Wharf. In no time at all it was locally known as Samuel Ellis's New Building.

There were always family events to divert him. His children, four daughters and one son, were either married or about to be. His daughter Catherine had married into the Westervelt family of New Jersey, and her husband served with the loyalist New Jersey Volunteers, until close to the end of the war. His son-in-law George Ryerson, married to daughter Elizabeth, served briefly as an ensign in the Volunteers as well. Two other daughters, Mary and Rachel,

had married prior to the revolution. And his son and namesake, Sam Ellis, Jr., was planning to wed Dorothy Walker. A few years later Sam sponsored the baptisms of some of his grandchildren at St. Paul's Chapel. Benjamin Moore officiated at the baptisms.

Charles Inglis, the rector of Trinity Church during the British occupation of New York, was passionately pro-British. He was secretly storing church records to take with him to Canada in the event the rebels won the war. Inglis knew that he and his wife were on the rebels' death list. When he did flee, he took with him not only church records but the entire congregation of two thousand.

The end of the long war came in September 1783. The patriots were triumphant in their revolt against Great Britain. Thirteen colonies had taken their first critical steps toward independent government and would face the problems of working out a democratic form of rule. On the eve of the great victory, the British and Tory supporters began their retreat. In November 1783 the British fleet sailed out of New York harbor carrying soldiers and their families. Following them, or boarding ships for Canada and the West Indies, were thousands of men, women, and children. In all, more than one hundred thousand loyalists fled the newly united colonies. The country lost able and talented people—scholars, clergymen, professionals, and administrators. Some were on death lists. Others feared physical punishment at the hands of victorious rebels; or they preferred English culture and politics; or they had family ties to England.

While the Stars and Stripes was hoisted over New York, General George Washington bid farewell to his officers at New York's Fraunces Tavern down at the Battery. They had fought side by side and experienced the violence and bloodshed of war, the freezing winters, hunger and despair, and finally victory.

Sam Ellis may have been part of the crowd that gathered to witness the scene. He would have observed the tall, six-foot-three-inch general leave the tavern and board a barge at Whitehall Ferry. Waving farewell to his weeping men, Washington set out for Annapolis to appear before Congress to resign his commission as army commander.

"To Be Sold ... An Island ..."

No sooner had the war ended than the little seaport exploded into feverish activity. But the revelry and excitement of the newly united colonies were not for Sam Ellis. He had waved farewell to his friends departing in the exodus of British forces. In the upheaval of a changing population, he remained home at One Greenwich Street.

As a known loyalist, Sam faced risks. Returning patriots, enraged at former enemies, were known to beat them up. A few were tarred and feathered. At the very least, loyalists were subjected to insult and ostracism. But Sam Ellis was only a small merchant, and he tried to slip quietly back into the life of the city.

It was not the same. No one abused him, and he held on to his home and property; but he had become an outsider. New neighbors moved into the empty houses nearby. They were very different from the old friends he had met and worshiped with at St. Paul's during the British occupation. Isaac Sears, a known radical revolutionary, a Son of Liberty, had taken over the large house around the corner at One Broad Way. Men and women who had fought against

31

the British flooded back with families to claim homes and land in the neighborhood. Many were poor and clamored for jobs and businesses. No longer did Sam have status in the community, and his fisheries suffered. Nor could he vote, for New York disfranchised all loyalists.

The seaport was not the same either. It was growing away from him, expanding so rapidly he could not keep up with it. His own street was being widened and extended past Cortlandt down to the foot of the Battery. And the old fort that shaped the tip of the town had been destroyed.

Sam Ellis, too, had to make changes, and among the first was to try to get rid of his little island. At times the island had been a nuisance, a site for accidents and missing boats. On one occasion he placed an ad in the newspaper:

BOAT FOUND ADRIFT, THE OWNER TO APPLY . . . AT MR. ELLIS'S ISLAND.

At another time, his kinsman William Ryley, while living on the island, rescued passengers of a sailboat hit by a squall. Often Sam picked up masts lost in the bay and had to find the owners.

Sam also had in mind moving to New Jersey. The idea had become more attractive with each passing year. Tory sympathizers were still flourishing in the rural areas. And his daughters Catherine and Elizabeth were living there with their families.

In 1785 Sam Ellis fully changed the direction of his life. He put his island up for sale and at the same time began to purchase land across the river. He announced the sale in Loudon's *New York Packet,* a town newspaper, on January 20, 1785. The ad read: [to be sold]

By Samuel Ellis, no 1 Greenwich Street, at the North River near the Bear Market, that pleasant situated island, called Oyster Island, lying in New York Bay, near Powles' [Paulus] Hook, together with all its improvements, which are considerable; also, two lots of ground, one at lower end of Queen Street, joining Luke's wharf, the other in Greenwich Street, between Petition [Partition] and Dey Streets, and a parcel of spars for masts, yards, brooms, bowsprits, etc. And a parcel of timber fit for pumps and building of docks; and a few barrels of excellent shad and herrings, and others of an inferior quality fit for shipping; and a few thousand of red herring of his own curing, that he will warrant to keep good in carrying to any part of the world, and a quality of twine which he will sell very low, which is the best sort of twine, for the tyke nets. Also a large Pleasure Sleigh, almost new.

Despite the many inducements, no one was interested in buying Sam Ellis's Island and it remained part of his estate. He concentrated his New Jersey landholdings along the Hudson River running west across the Salt Meadows and marshes into the fertile valley of the Hackensack River. By 1790 he had ended up with hundreds of acres of woodland, orchards, farmhouses, sheds and barns, cows and horses. A year later, he came into possession of another one hundred ninety acres in Newburgh, New York, also bordering the Hudson. To add to his wealth, he inherited property in Albany County in 1792. Sam Ellis had become land rich, the owner of valuable property along both sides of the Hudson River.

His New York property was extended in September 1793 by a grant that gave him or his heirs rights of land under the water near his lots. It was known as liquid real estate.

33

If he wished, he could add landfill along the water's edge and create another street. The same grant gave him outright "that part of [church] estate called Oyster or Ellis Island," confirming his ownership.

For many years William Ryley lived on the island in a makeshift dwelling. He continued to use it as a fishery and at the same time protected the island from marauders.

Though Samuel Ellis had moved to New Jersey and lived the life of a farmer, he was aware of the continuing excitement in New York City. It had become the first capital of the nation. Elaborate celebrations on river and land honored the country's first president, George Washington.

Packed with men, women, and children, every ship in working condition floated down the river to join the inaugural festivities on April 30, 1789. Schooners sailed in from Albany, Kingston, and Newburgh. Packet boats arrived from Boston. Every vehicle was on the road—oxcarts, wagons, and carriages loaded with people from small towns in Pennsylvania and New Jersey. People slept in tents on open fields.

Sam Ellis's old neighborhood rang out with the revelry of pealing church bells, music, boat horns, and hurrahs of excitement from hoarse throats. After the inauguration ceremony, the president, surrounded by a crush of supporters,

walked with other officials to St. Paul's Chapel for divine blessing. Dressed simply in a dark suit, white silk stockings, and buckled shoes, his hair powdered white and tied back, he entered the church and knelt in prayer. Years before, Sam Ellis had worshiped in that chapel and had brought his grandchildren there to be baptized. Now, across the river, amid the leftover factions of conservative pro-British loyalists, he stood on the Jersey shore watching the pageantry.

Extravagant dances, balls, and dinners for the social elite continued to celebrate the presence of President George Washington in the seaport city. At their home on 3 Cherry Street, a three-story, red-brick building, Martha Washington played hostess to glittering socialites.

By August 1790 the president had departed from New York to a new governmental site and home. But the city continued to thrive. It had grown into a financial center of wealth and prestige. Everywhere new businesses were springing up. The waterways hummed with commerce. Three months after the British evacuation, the newly united country initiated the China trade, sending the *Empress of China,* the world's first clipper ship, to Canton. U.S.-built vessels carried cargoes of rice, tobacco, wheat, and fish abroad. They returned, as in the old days, not only with manufactured goods but with newcomers. New York City had become a major port for immigrants entering the United States.

No regulations hindered these new arrivals, for everyone was free to come. From its earliest days the seaport had been an international city, resounding with many languages.

As the country expanded, taking over Indian territory, it needed people to work the land. The federal government offered free transportation, food, acreage, and farm tools to both natives and immigrants who would settle the prairies and wilderness. And there were many who were eager to meet the challenge. The French Huguenots settled north of the seaport and created a village, New Rochelle. The Germans moved into Pennsylvania; the Scotch-Irish settled the Shenandoah Valley; the Swedes farmed the Delaware Valley.

From small beginnings, the nation could count a population of more than three million in its first census in 1790. The residents of New York had grown in number from fifteen hundred to over thirty thousand.

In the noise and tumult of change, who cared about Ellis's Island? Did anyone even know it existed? Isolated, the island lay peacefully in the Hudson and would have remained that way but for its location in Upper New York Bay.

The young nation had serious matters before it. One of them concerned the defense of its long coastline. To protect the crucial harbor of New York from enemy attack, military strategists envisioned possible dangers. They said enemy ships could sail through the Narrows, the sea channel between Brooklyn and Staten Island, into Upper New York Bay and thus gain access to the northern territories via the Hudson River.

With this threatening image in mind, the strategists formulated defense plans. Nearby Governors Island had already been fortified. Bedloe's had also been garrisoned. Now the army announced that Sam Ellis's Island was vital to the defense of the United States.

In the early 1790s the government received verbal permission from Sam Ellis to build a garrison on his island. Perhaps he no longer much cared about that patch of land.

By 1793 he was not in good health, and his spirits were low. He was in deep mourning over the deaths of two of his children. His only son, Sam Ellis, Jr., died in 1792 and his daughter Mary, too, died after a brief illness. Left behind in both families were spouses and children to be cared for.

Sam also worried about his wife, Mary, and his three remaining daughters and their growing families. To add to his responsibilities, his daughter Catherine was pregnant and separated from her husband. He felt he had to provide for them as well as for friends and other kinspeople. He wrote his will carefully, making provisions for wife, children, grandchildren, and friends.

His first concern was for his daughter Catherine. In his will he stipulated that her child, if it was a boy, should be baptized Samuel Ellis. To that child should go Oyster, or Sam Ellis's, Island with all the buildings thereon. If, on the

other hand, the child was a girl, that child would simply inherit a portion of her mother's estate.

Sam Ellis did not live long after he wrote his will. He died on July 4, 1794. His will was probated, and when Catherine Ellis Westervelt gave birth to a son, he was duly baptized Samuel Ellis and became the owner of his grandfather's island. When, however, the child died in infancy, the island reverted to the Ellis estate. Its legal ownership remained clouded for years because of the confusion surrounding the early death of Catherine's son.

And not only the legal ownership was questioned. In addition, city, state, and federal governments, as well as the army and navy, became involved in a maze of claims over who had authority over the island.

In 1798 New York City stepped in and converted the island into a recruiting station. Stone buildings were erected to house and train soldiers. The encampment was officially called "A General Rendezvous for the Recruits of the Corps of Artilleries and Engineers in the U.S. Army." The long, intricate title hardly fitted the desolate piece of land. Its isolation and lack of entertainment facilities for young people caused trouble. A few recruits took off without official leave. To get them back, the army appealed to the public in newspaper ads:

TEN DOLLARS REWARD, FOR APPREHENDING OF THOMAS RYNE OF ARTILLERIES AND ENGINEERS, WHO DESERTED FROM RENDEZVOUS ON ELLIS ISLAND.

Two years later, in 1800, the federal government won jurisdiction over Governors, Bedloe's, and Ellis islands. But Ellis Island was still privately owned. That contradiction seemed resolved when Samuel Ellis Ryerson, the son of daughter Elizabeth, sold the island to a neighbor named

John Berry. Berry then sold it to New York State, and in 1810 New York State sold the island to the federal government. But the controversy never abated, for the Ellis family disputed Sam Ryerson's right to sell the island. Because of the continuing legal confusion, the federal government for many years had no clear title to that particular 3.3-acre bit of land.

Nevertheless, Ellis Island was finally approved as a fortification. On it was placed a parapet for three tiers of circular guns, making the island part of the defense of the bay from Paulus Hook to the Narrows.

While legal problems continued, the U.S. government was involved in critical events with England and France that culminated in the War of 1812. Freedom of the seas had been disrupted for years because of the battles between Napoleon of France and the British Empire. Caught in their wars was the United States. Finally, on June 1, 1812, the United States declared war on Great Britain. Until the signing of the peace in 1814, the life of the seaport of New York was at a standstill. And though none of the guns had been fired during the war, it was agreed that the fortifications on the islands of Upper New York Bay discouraged a British invasion.

To honor two American officers killed in the war of 1812, Ellis Island was renamed Fort Gibson. Fort Gibson it remained for the following eighty years, a site for random executions of pirates, or soldiers who threatened the life of an officer.

In 1843, Fort Gibson was designated a storage depot for ammunition. A naval magazine was constructed and filled with explosives. To the populated areas of New Jersey, New York, Staten Island, and Brooklyn, the arsenal meant danger, a threat to their lives and property.

"... a general invitation to the people of the world ..."

Ellis Island was only a speck in the national concerns of the United States. From the first days of independence, the country had visions of greatness. Through annexation, dispossession of the Indians, and war, the government appropriated the land between the Atlantic and Pacific oceans. By 1850 the U.S. flag waved over the continent from ocean to ocean.

New York City had developed into an influential financial and social center. Drawn by its commerce, people also enjoyed the theaters, dances, clubs, and literary talks. A steady flow of immigrants added to its population and sophisticated air.

Immigrants not only endowed the city with excitement and variety, they also aided in the country's expansion. European settlers had created the country in their image in colonial days. They had urged others to join them. Except for periods of war and economic depression, the steady flow of peoples continued. Between 1820 and the outbreak

of the Civil War in 1861, more than six million immigrants arrived, the majority from northern and western Europe.

Families left European homes and poured into the United States because earlier immigrants sent word that jobs were available and land was cheap; that there were no taxes and no army draft. Others were lured by U.S. agencies that had established offices in Europe to attract newcomers. These agencies had posters hung in public squares and ads placed in journals and newspapers. They advised on where to settle, signed up laborers, and offered cheap tickets for passage on ships.

Such campaigns, coupled with the hard lives of the European poor, enticed millions to the new country. A popular ballad of the time describes the situation:

> Of all the mighty nations in the East or in the West
> This glorious Yankee nation is the greatest and the best;
> We have room for all creation and our banner is unfurled,
> Here's a general invitation to the people of the world.

Come along, come along, make no delay,
Come from every nation, come from every way;
Our lands are broad enough, don't be alarmed,
For Uncle Sam is rich enough to give us all a farm.

Europeans made their way to ports and boarded any ship that could make the ocean crossing. They packed into the ships' lowest decks with their valuables tied up in bed sheets or straw baskets. They squeezed into squalid bunks in airless quarters and ate food that often rotted during the passage.

In the early years they traveled fifteen weeks; then, as shipping improved, the journey was cut to ten weeks, then six, and finally four. In 1818 packet ships initiated regular crossings that took only twenty-three days. By 1838 steamships made the crossings in fifteen days. Too poor for such luxury, however, most continued to travel on old sailing vessels. They could pay as little as ten dollars for a passage ticket. In a steady stream millions uprooted themselves, leaving behind homes and friends, their spinning wheels and tools.

New York became the main gateway for immigrants. On any day the harbor was filled with ships flying flags of foreign countries. Before immigrants could rest up from the difficult ocean crossing, they were put onto barges and ferried from ships directly to shore. If lucky, they were met by families and friends. If unlucky, they fell into the hands of hustlers who robbed them of money and possessions.

In a major wave of immigration from 1820 to 1861, most of the newcomers joined native settlers in the westward migration. They traveled over the Appalachian Mountain chain, boarded ships on swift-running rivers, and drove covered wagons over thousands of miles of prairies. Like conquerors, they annexed the land.

The expansion of the country and immigration were linked together. The larger the territory, the more people were needed to plant the soil. Wherever the immigrants settled they brought energy and drive. They came with technical experience learned in industrial England, and with skills as farmers, dyers, weavers, and furniture makers. They brought knowledge of medicine, science, and law.

While Europeans arrived voluntarily, black Africans did not. As slaves, they were forced to contribute their labor. They built plantations and reared their young for the slave market. None of the benefits were theirs.

The country became a patchwork of natives and new-comers. Its inhabitants sang songs in many tongues. The Indians, fighting the invasion of their land, sang songs of resistance. The African slaves sang songs of sorrow. The Germans brought Bach to the Ohio Valley. The Norwegians and Swedes sang ballads in Minnesota. The Irish played their jigs in New York and Boston.

Though many lives were blighted by the uprooting, most people were not disappointed. They were doing better than in the old country. Education was free; land was cheap; religious toleration made possible churches of many denominations. They could settle down or pull up stakes and start over.

The traditional policy of the country, dating from colonial times, had been one of unrestricted immigration. In the absence of a uniform federal policy after the Revolution, each state regulated immigration its own way. New York tried to exclude criminals, paupers, and diseased aliens. The regulation of this policy, placed in the hands of the police, failed. For a short time the state imposed a small head tax on each arrival; that was declared unconstitutional by the U.S. Supreme Court.

In 1848 large numbers of poor Chinese were brought to the West Coast under contract to work the fields during the gold rush. And in the decade of the 1850s a million and a half Europeans arrived. Among them were Germans and Poles whose entry at first caused little opposition. But then Irish Catholics, fleeing the terrible potato famine, flooded the country. Uneducated, they filled jobs for common labor, building tunnels, bridges, and canals. Too poor to make the westward migration, they crowded into eastern cities, Boston and New York, where they entered into local politics and became a powerful force. Their firm religious beliefs appeared threatening and brought on the first major anti-immigrant outbreaks in the East. Protestants, fearing for the survival of their faith, opposed the continuing influx of Irish Catholics. Workers protested the competition for jobs. Others complained about the deterioration of the cities into immigrant ghettos.

Antiforeign feelings were not new. They were there from

the country's beginning, but they had never been significantly aroused. Now, in response to the influx of poor Irish in the East and poor Chinese in the West, antiforeign movements sprang up. They were fed by concepts of nativism, a form of nationalism, that preached opposition to immigrants in favor of the native born.

The most active group developed in the early 1850s into the Know-Nothing Party. In secret rituals and ceremonies, members committed themselves to make the country safe for native Americans only; to fight Catholicism, to rid the country of foreign-born liberals and radicals, and to demand naturalization for aliens only after twenty-one years' residency. In a slogan, "Americans shall rule America," they attacked the Irish influence in politics.

Their power was temporarily broken by the larger issue tearing the country apart—the issue of slavery. Nevertheless, simmering resistance to immigration created an

urgency to regulate, in some way, the steady flow of foreigners.

In response to the pressures, New York State set up its first processing center. In 1855 it took over a large building in New York City called Castle Garden and placed it under the direction of the State Emigration Commission.

There was no simple solution to the problems of immigration. The country, on the edge of the great industrial revolution, needed cheap labor to lay railway tracks, build factories, and work complex machines, using new energy sources—steam power and electricity.

In the midst of raging national issues, local issues won headlines in newspapers. In New York City Sam Ellis's Island was again in the news. The public felt increasingly threatened by the huge amounts of ammunition stored on the island. During the Civil War, heavy guns and explosives had been installed. Such large stockpiles of munitions were a danger to crowded cities, claimed the New York *Sun* and *Harper's Weekly*. The ammunition was in "immediate danger of exploding and destroying the area," said one headline. Local politicians took the fight to the United States Congress. They insisted that Ellis Island be emptied of explosives.

The presence of an arsenal on Sam Ellis's Island was not the only local issue to capture public attention. Castle Garden, the immigration center, was also in trouble.

Castle Garden

Ellis Island and Castle Garden were within sight of each other in Upper New York Bay. Both had been part of the strategic defense of the harbor during the War of 1812.

Ellis Island, rising gently out of the sea, was the creation of a long-ago geological age. Castle Garden, originally designed as a fortress, was built on an artificially made island off the southwest tip of the Battery. Called Fort Clinton in its early days, it was an enormous red sandstone building, thick-walled, octagonal in shape, and connected to the mainland by a drawbridge. Twenty-eight heavy cannon poked through its walls. It looked like a "large red wart" at the entrance to Manhattan, commented a contemporary.

Like Ellis Island, now Fort Gibson, Fort Clinton never fired a shot. Still, a huge fortress blocking the face of New York made the country feel secure. At the end of the War of 1812 Fort Clinton became useless, and the federal government ceded it to New York City in 1823.

What could New York do with the hulking structure? First, it was leased to private entrepreneurs who put the fort through a series of elaborate facelifts and renamed it Castle Garden. Little could soften its red sandstone exterior and harsh shape. But over the years additions of gardens, fountains, promenades, and brilliant, fanciful lighting made it a glittering showplace.

It opened as a resort and restaurant and then moved on to become the city's official reception center. Once, thousands turned out to welcome the French hero of the American Revolution, General Lafayette. A few years later President Andrew Jackson was honored. In the 1840s, in another stage of its transformation, the structure was roofed over and enlarged into an arena seating six thousand, making it the largest hall in the country.

Castle Garden, now permanently connected to the Battery by more landfill, became the city's major entertainment center. Operas, concerts, theaters, fairs, exhibits, and fireworks attracted thousands of visitors. Audiences cheered the performances of the Italian Opera Company. They went wild over Jenny Lind, the Swedish Nightingale, who gave

a series of well-publicized concerts in the 1850s. There, too, Spanish dancer Lola Montez and European ballerina Carlotta Grisi made their U.S. debuts.

Despite ingenuity and fanciful trim, Castle Garden did not succeed financially. The building was handed back to the city and was therefore available to the New York State Emigration Commission during the anti-immigration furor.

In 1855 the commission transformed Castle Garden into the state's first immigration center. Space was divided into medical-examination rooms, offices for personnel, and information booths. Outdoors a high wooden fence encircled the building. Thus, a redesigned Castle Garden became the gateway to the United States.

From transatlantic ships anchored offshore, barges transported aliens to the red sandstone building for registration. Between 1855 and 1890 about eight million came through its doors. All over the world, popular wisdom claimed that whoever set foot in Castle Garden had touched U.S. soil. Except for a temporary lull during the Civil War, 1861–65, aliens poured through the "Nation's Gateway" into official channels for settlement in New York or migration to the interior by train or boat.

Procedures were brief. Immigrants were checked for infectious diseases and criminal records, and to determine if they had come for purposes of prostitution. Such aliens were, supposedly, to be shipped back to their homelands. But nearly everyone slipped through the loose regulations. Registration became a joke. Some immigrants bought their way into the country through bribery, paying off inspectors. Sick people, criminals, those with no resources arrived and were also admitted.

While there were immigrants who took advantage of loose and corrupt inspection, many more were victims. In their exhaustion and ignorance of U.S. ways, their possessions were easily stolen. Or job brokers rushed them into work contracts before they had their bearings.

Publicity about the laxity of procedures led to increased opposition to immigration after the Civil War. Building on the Know-Nothing protests, new voices claimed that the low breed of newcomers was coarsening the native stock and destroying the intellectual growth of the country.

Labor's opposition also increased. Their gains were weakened, labor leaders said, when immigrants worked long hours at low wages. Further, they claimed that immigrants grabbed the few jobs available during economic depressions.

On the Pacific Coast, where Chinese had been brought over as contract labor to work the gold mines and railroads, labor and nativists fought against their unchecked entrance into the United States. "The Chinese Must Go!" became a fighting slogan, especially during the economic crisis of 1873, which brought soaring unemployment.

The mounting clamor to limit immigration forced the federal government to intercede. Congress, already swayed by effective lobbying, took the first step in 1875 when it prohibited the entrance of prostitutes and criminals. By 1882 serious restrictions were enacted into federal law. Categories of people to be excluded were expanded to include the sick, paupers, alcoholics, and anyone who might become a public charge. That law also blocked the entrance of Chinese for a period of ten years. By 1885 importation of all contract labor was declared illegal.

Labor demanded further restrictions, leading the battle for a literacy test as a criterion for admission to the country to limit the influx of the uneducated. Pressure mounted and restrictionists were gaining headway. But nothing se-

riously blocked the flow of immigration. A new wave of aliens began to arrive from Italy and Eastern Europe. While restrictionists whipped up public outrage, publisher Joseph Pulitzer in 1887 used his newspaper, the *Telegram*, to expose the shoddy procedures at Castle Garden that enabled "undesirables" to enter the country. He also pointed to the shortage of officials in the face of soaring immigration. In 1888 alone, 76 percent of the half million who arrived were processed at Castle Garden. An impossible situation existed. One official claimed that the whole system was a "perfect farce."

At about the same time, the storage of explosives on Ellis Island was getting wide publicity. The newspaper, the *Sun*, exposed the dangers to the community. "New York Still Standing. The Powder Magazine not yet struck by lightning," was a lead article in May 1876. New Jersey congressmen, pressured by residents, urged the army and the navy to remove the explosives from the island.

These campaigns for immediate change linked the two islands together. Castle Garden was attacked for inefficient immigration procedures. Ellis Island was considered a public danger for its storage of munitions.

Under mounting pressure, the federal government finally acknowledged its responsibility for regulating immigration. It also determined the need for a new, federally supervised processing center and created a committee to search for a suitable site. Bedloe's was considered. But that island had already been promised as the location for a statue that had been undertaken by the sculptor Auguste Bartholdi on behalf of France.

Joseph Pulitzer, still carrying on his campaign against the stores of ammunition on Ellis Island, directed attention to its availability. In quick succession, congressional leg-

islation canceled the use of Ellis Island as an arsenal and called for the prompt removal of its powder magazine.

Ellis Island, no longer serving a useful purpose, was now available as a possible immigration center. Government officials looked the island over but they were not impressed. They saw a flat island lying low in shallow water, isolated, difficult to reach. Nevertheless, in the absence of other suggestions, President Benjamin Harrison signed a resolution on April 11, 1890, declaring Ellis Island a federal immigration depot. The same act placed Ellis Island under the auspices of the U.S. Treasury Department.

Immigration procedures were brought to a halt at Castle Garden in 1890. During the following two years, while Ellis Island was being redesigned, immigrants were processed at the Barge Office. (Castle Garden, taken over by the Park Department, was opened as an Aquarium in 1896 and operated until 1941. In 1946 it was designated a national monument.)

Samuel Ellis, the wholesale dealer in fish in the seaport of New York, had been dead almost one hundred years when the island he once owned made his name part of history. Around the world millions would talk about Ellis Island, the gateway to the United States.

Ellis Island

Fifteen-year-old Annie Moore of County Cork, Ireland, was the first immigrant to set foot on Ellis Island. Immediately after her came her two brothers, Tom and Joe. It was New Year's Day, January 1, 1892.

The children had stayed behind in Ireland in the care of an aunt when their parents, Matt and Mary Moore, migrated to the United States. After three long years in the new country, the Moores sent a special letter back home. Enclosed were three tickets for their children for passage on the ship *Nevada.*

After ten days at sea, the *Nevada* sailed through the Narrows and reached New York harbor at night. Annie and her younger brothers were gathering together their belongings and getting ready to go through immigration procedures, along with hundreds of other poor passengers confined to the lower decks, or steerage. Only cabin-class passengers, standing at the rail, could see an awesome sight: From Bedloe's Island the Statue of Liberty, her torch lighted, dominated the bay. She had been unveiled in 1886 as Liberty Enlightening the World.

On the morning after arrival, while the *Nevada* was anchored in the bay, physicians boarded the ship for quarantine inspection of the passengers in cabin class, to make sure no one with an infectious disease was entering the country. After that, these passengers were permitted to leave the ship.

This special morning, a small tugboat drew up alongside the *Nevada*. Annie, Tom, Joe, and several others were lowered into it and ferried across the bay. Waiting on Ellis Island were Matt and Mary Moore and members of the press. Reporters wrote up the story. They described the joy and excitement of Matt and Mary Moore as the tug drew nearer. "There's little Annie—and little Tom and little Joe," the Moores were said to have shouted.

The Moores hoped that Annie's arrival on January 1, also her birthday, would bring the family good luck. Before the parents could fold the children in their arms, they witnessed the ceremony opening Ellis Island as a federal immigration center.

Commissioner Weber and other officials greeted Annie as she stepped off the tug. After he said a few words, he handed Annie a shining ten-dollar gold piece as a souvenir. Her two brothers followed after her, and then, along with hundreds of others, Annie lined up to be registered as an immigrant. She became one of the millions to be admitted to the United States. On its first day, Ellis Island processed more than two thousand newcomers.

Renovations to the island had not yet been completed when it opened as an immigration center. Workers had put in long, hard hours for two years to make major changes. Sam Ellis's Island was expanded, reshaped, and replanted. Its original 3.3 acres was doubled. Ships from foreign ports had poured their ballast into cribs for landfill dug around the island. Ellis Island became the most international piece of land on earth as well as a receiving center for people from around the world.

Workmen had also dredged a twelve-foot channel for docks and slips. Old stone and brick buildings were converted into dormitories and storage bins. New structures included a large two-story central building, a hospital, a boiler room, laundry and electric plants, artesian wells, and cisterns. It took an additional five years before the last workers had finished their jobs. All the new construction was made of wood. On June 15, 1897 the buildings were declared completed, and the last of the workmen wrapped up their tools and left.

That night a fire broke out a little past midnight in the

tower of the main hall. The roof collapsed, and flames shot through the new wooden buildings. Everything was gutted, every structure, and all the Castle Garden records were burned. A few stone buildings, remnants of older days, tumbled in the heat of the flames.

Fireboats, police patrols, and all available craft swiftly made their way to the island. They safely evacuated the two to three hundred staff and immigrants lodged there. Many of the immigrants were detainees, but a few had been hospitalized for serious illnesses.

The flames, visible for miles around, lighted up the harbor. From the Battery, where Sam Ellis had once stood and looked across the Hudson to his little island, throngs of onlookers now watched the sparks shoot out of the river.

For days acrid smells hung over the headlands of New Jersey. Ellis Island was a charred, gloomy ruin. Here and there stood a stone wall, a bulwark of Fort Gibson days.

Not only buildings and records lay buried in the ruins;

the spirit of Sam Ellis's tiny island was gone. But fire wasn't the only culprit. People had intervened in the natural life of the island, changing its ecology. For many years the Hudson River had been a dumping ground, filled with debris from large cities. Its ecology too had changed. Ellis Island was no longer a shelter for sea birds. Its rich beds of oysters and shellfish had been destroyed. But despite years of landfill and construction, the island lay forever low in the water, its original contours still visible. Now, Ellis Island would have a new image. Brick, stone, and ironwork buildings would reflect the power and force of the United States in the industrial age.

Ellis Island had registered close to a million and a half immigrants during the five and a half years prior to the fire. While immigrants were temporarily processed at the Barge Office on the Battery after the fire, elaborate blueprints were drawn up for a new federal immigration center.

Again, the island was stretched into a new shape. In

1897 it was a 10-acre site. In 1934 it had been extended to 27.54 acres. Instead of one island there were now three islands connected to each other at first by bridges, then by landfill.

No matter how much Ellis Island expanded, its facilities remained inadequate to handle the restless influx of millions. Word had spread into the rural backwaters and urban alleys of the world that the United States was the land of opportunity. And people came in a huge procession that changed the face of Europe and created new forces in the United States.

The largest wave of immigration, between 1892 and 1924, brought seventeen million through Ellis Island. The number peaked after 1901. They came mostly from Southern and Eastern Europe—Poles, Italians, Russian Jews, Rumanians, Hungarians, Turks, and Greeks. They had made their way to European ports, to Hamburg, Piraeus, Marseilles, and Naples, crowding into the steerage of oceangoing vessels for the hard crossing. In the year 1907 alone, more than one million three hundred thousand aliens arrived. On a single day, April 17, 1907, eleven thousand awaited their turn to be processed.

Like people before them, most came to escape hard lives. They left behind poverty, the army, religious persecution, hunger, and despair. What did they have to lose? A spirit of optimism lighted their minds with dreams, giving them the courage to face an unknown world.

Their ships took them through the Narrows and dropped anchor in Upper New York Bay. The first sight to greet them was the Statue of Liberty. Hidden in its shadow was Ellis Island, its flat expanse protected by a seawall. After quarantine inspection, steerage passengers were placed in barges and ferried to the island. They remained crowded together for hours on these open, flat boats, protected neither from hot sun nor freezing cold. They were an exhausted, bewildered mass of people, gripped by fear. Would they pass the examinations? Would the doctor notice a lame leg, an inflamed eye? Would they be shipped back?

From their barges at the quay, immigrants faced an enormous central building called the Registry Hall. Made of brick and limestone, with arched doorways and a huge dome over its two stories, it looked as if built for eternity. Four turreted pinnacles arising from its corners gave the building height and visibility. Within, three enormous crystal and brass fixtures hung from the domed ceiling. Both ceiling and floor were tiled.

The first floor held the waiting room, baggage facilities, transportation offices, money changers, post office, and restaurant. On the second floor were the registration and examination rooms, and administration offices. Other buildings included a chapel, hospital, dormitories, child-care centers, powerhouses, and bathhouses. New facilities were added as the need increased. In all, thirty-three structures covered Ellis Island. It also had its own ferry slip.

Whether Ellis Island was six acres or twenty-seven, procedures did not much vary. Each immigrant was tagged with two numbers. These told inspectors the page and line on the ship's list, called manifest sheets, where the immigrant's name could be found. Slowly lines of people walked across the quay and into the Great Hall for examinations, which took place night and day. From the first days, laughter and tears echoed through the vaulted building. People shouted and cried in forty different languages. For each language an interpreter was standing by.

After dropping off their baggage on the first floor (which

many feared to do), arrivals formed lines leading up the center staircase. On the second floor medical personnel examined them for a wide spectrum of diseases ranging from poor eyesight to mental illness. Although experienced doctors could give only brief examinations to the endless lines of aliens, they quickly spotted deformities, skin diseases, and other telltale symptoms. They were on the alert for trachoma, an infectious eye disease that could lead to blindness. Here, the dreaded eye examinations took place. Using a metal instrument, doctors turned eyelids inside out, often a painful procedure.

When there was doubt, physicians put a chalk mark on the immigrant's back or shoulder. The letter *E* meant eyestrain; *H* signified heart disease; *X* stood for mental defects; *L* for lameness. Those detained were directed to wired detention centers. Families cried out in horror when a relative was isolated in one of these cages. About two percent, or about a quarter of a million aliens, were ultimately returned to their countries of origin.

When illnesses were curable, immigrants were directed to dormitories or hospitals, or they were sent to bathhouses to have lice removed. Many were angered by the implication that they had arrived carrying these parasites. They claimed they picked up lice on Ellis Island when forced to sleep on filthy benches and floors because of the overcrowding. Immigrants like Mary Zuk, who arrived in 1912, told her side of the story. "Ellis Island was lousy. Lousy. Bugs all over," she said. Others resented the "humiliating physical, mental and moral examinations." They were "pushed around, literally pushed," many complained.

The vast majority, about 80 percent, faced another hurdle after they passed the medical examinations. They were directed through passageways into long aisles to be ques-

tioned by legal inspectors. In two minutes, officials behind large desks shot a list of thirty questions at each immigrant, checking answers against the ship's manifest. Steamship companies were required to register immigrants' vital facts before they sold tickets.

Inspectors asked: name, birthplace, age, who paid for passage, plans for jobs and housing, family or sponsors. "Are you an anarchist? Are you a polygamist? Do you have a criminal record?"

Those who gave unsatisfactory answers were pulled from the line, chalk-marked "SI," and held for further questioning by the Board of Special Inquiry.

Finally, for millions there were "landing cards." Fears and anxieties fled. Clutching the precious cards, they fell into the waiting arms of families and friends. Or social-agency staffs took them in charge. They were ferried the mile across the Hudson to New York City or a few hundred feet to the New Jersey shore. Thus millions began their lives in another country.

They told and retold their stories, and handed them down to their children. They kept the words alive—Ellis Island. It meant America.

There was a dark side. Some lost their focus and did not survive. They sickened over the hardships endured in steerage, over their fears of rejection, and deprivation of identity. Bewildered, they discovered that their native languages seemed useless—they could not make themselves heard or understood. Some went mad. Others, to put an end to their pain, committed suicide.

To many in the United States the immigrants from eastern Europe and the Mediterranean were a shabby, bizarre, ugly group of people. They complained that the newcomers were too short, too swarthy, too poor—generally, of a low order. Their languages were incomprehensible, nothing short of gibberish. Nativists who favored Nordic types found them "deficient."

Others, however, saw their beauty. What a lucky country, they said, to receive a procession of the people of the world—people with skills and talents, eager to give and eager to learn. They brought to their new homeland "gifts precious and golden as wheat," in the words of poet Pablo Neruda.

Augustus Sherman, a clerk who worked at Ellis Island, was also a photographer. He and others, notably photographer Lewis Hine, recorded the immigrants' arrival. A series of simple portraits reveal the dignity and appeal of the newcomers: bearded men of eastern Europe, dark, deep-

1907

set eyes in sad faces, wearing stiff black hats and stiff black frock coats; dark-eyed people of Italy; women in blouses, long skirts, kerchiefs covering their heads; a Hungarian woman and her four children wearing long dresses and kerchiefs made of the same cotton plaid cloth; a Rumanian woman surrounded by her four young daughters; children curiously alive in their stillness. There are Syrians, Russians, Hungarians, and tattooed German stowaways.

Most of these millions did not go west to farm. The frontier was closed. They filled the factories with their cheap labor power. They worked in the coal mines, wielded a pickax, split rails, converted ore to steel, dug roads, built tunnels and bridges. Women and children put their labor into textile mills and the clothing industry. They worked in firetrap factories, twelve to fourteen hours a day, for low wages. They lived in slums and died of tuberculosis.

When they saw what they produced, they asked for a fair return on their labor. They organized, marched, and pushed at the power structure. The country had to make room for them, give them decent housing, fair wages, and their just rights in the courts of law.

Wherever they lived, organizations sprang up to help them. On the Lower East Side, the first stop for most of the immigrants coming through Ellis Island, the Henry Street Settlement House offered education and health care. Under the direction of Lillian Wald, nurses began the movement for public-health services, housing and jobs. Other settlements, cultural clubs, charitable and religious organizations, and a handful of philanthropists tried to cushion the impact of industrial society on dislocated people. Many reformers offered views on how to change their condition.

To become successful, immigrants were urged to assimilate into the American way of life. Reluctantly they merged their customs into native patterns. They contributed their languages, literature, their ways of preparing food, their dances and songs. Within many, however, traditions lingered. They carried the habits of the old country into the new.

At the same time they discovered the benefits of their adopted land. Free education meant their children could learn a profession, enter business, run for political office. And while they were adjusting, opponents to further immigration grew stronger.

As the country moved inexorably into the violence of World War I, the forces urging "restriction" became victorious.

The Closed Door

From the country's earliest days there have been people eager to slam the door shut against newcomers. Sometimes these forces were small and met in secret. At other times they burst into the open and swayed the public with attacks and denunciations against the foreign-born.

As early as 1798 the young country passed the Alien and Sedition Acts, which gave the president special powers. He could deport any alien he considered "dangerous to the peace and safety of the United States," or anyone stirring up trouble against the president and Congress. These acts were declared unconstitutional two years later.

Over the years pressure to limit immigration would surface. This was especially so during times of economic depression when jobs were scarce.

In the 1850s there had been the nativist attacks against the Irish Catholics, Germans, and Chinese. By the 1870s and 1880s restrictive legislation was signed into law. Not only did these acts curb immigration, but often they were discriminatory. They singled out national origin as a basis for rejection. In 1882 the Chinese Exclusion Act restricted for ten years the admission of the Chinese. This restriction was later made permanent. In 1885 the Contract Labor Law struck a blow at the importation of cheap labor. In 1888 illegal aliens could be deported.

By 1891, when immigration was put under federal supervision, propaganda for restriction sharply escalated. Scholars had joined the furor against the incoming tide of people. Harvard graduates formed the Immigration Restriction League. Others joined the American Protective Association. Anthropologists and sociologists evolved "scientific" theories about race and disease. They said poverty and crime were inherited characteristics. They talked about the "dregs of civilization," and the wretched inferior people of eastern Europe. They pointed the finger at the Jews and in a wave of anti-Semitism urged their exclusion from the country. In 1896, according to Senator Henry Cabot Lodge, people such as the Jews, Poles, Hungarians, Greeks, and Asiatics were a danger to the "mental and moral qualities" of the American people.

By the time the United States entered World War I in 1917, it was on a course toward repression and intimidation in domestic policy. A wave of terror settled over the country. Danger was seen in every foreign-born group. Conservative and nativist forces accused aliens of enemy nations of being spies or, at the very least, of being disloyal. Racism, anti-Semitism, and anti-Catholicism flared in every community.

The Russian Revolution of 1917 further deepened the already exaggerated fears. The specter of communism haunted government and industry. They saw "Russian agents" and "communist infiltrators" in every dissenting voice, especially during periods of labor unrest.

In the Red Scare that overtook the country after the war,

thousands of innocent people were rounded up and jailed. Radical labor leaders often met a worse fate. They were kidnapped, beaten, and lynched. Many Russian-born persons were arrested, thrown into jail overnight, and then released.

Despite arrests and beatings workers continued to demand improved working conditions. A series of vigorous strikes involving more than four million spread across the land in 1919. Fears of class warfare blew up into wild proportions.

To put an end to the labor upheaval, Attorney General Mitchell A. Palmer directed raids against labor leaders and dissenters with special emphasis on the foreign-born. His crusade spawned arrests all over the country. In Seattle, where a militant strike was taking place, the mayor, in surprise raids, had fifty-four alien labor leaders arrested. They were taken to prison trains and shipped East. In many towns and cities similar raids and arrests were taking place.

These adjudged "enemies" of the United States ended up at Ellis Island. The island became their detention center until ships could return them to the countries of their birth. Among them were English, Norwegian, Russian, Swedish, Finnish, and Dutch foreign-born. A few were glad to return to their native countries. Many, torn from families and homes, fought to stay and started lawsuits against the government. One newspaper called it the "great deportation delirium" of 1919–20.

Like a barometer, Ellis Island registered the changes in the country. Immigration was on the wane, and a new set of officers were trained to police detainees and deportees.

The anarchist Emma Goldman, outspoken in opposition to World War I, was one of those returned to Russia, her native country. In her autobiography she describes her sense of loss. "To be driven out of the land I called my own, where I had toiled and suffered for years, was not a cheerful prospect," she said.

Miss Goldman was arrested in December 1919, and taken to Ellis Island. There she was placed in a room with two other women, who had been members of an organization called the Union of Russian Workers. Little had changed since her Castle Garden experience, Miss Goldman wrote. She was "finger-printed, photographed and tabulated." Two weeks later she was rushed out of her cell onto a barge that transferred her to the *S.S. Buford.* In the morning mist the vessel set sail. Receding in the background was the Statue of Liberty.

In the trauma of war and the postwar period, it was easy to promote antialien legislation. Restrictionists won another victory when Congress passed a law calling for a literacy test in 1917. It judged a person's competence to enter the country on an ability to read and write one's native language. Though a similar bill had been vetoed by three previous presidents, this one was passed over the veto of President Wilson. The act struck a blow directly at the uneducated poor of southern and eastern Europe.

That year, an "Asian Barred Zone" cut off immigration from most of Asia and the Pacific Islands, including Siam, India, and IndoChina. A clause added to the bill excluded stowaways from entry. (In 1921 more than thirty-five hundred had hidden on incoming ships.)

The restrictions notwithstanding, hundreds of thousands continued to pour into the country. To block the relentless flow, Congress in 1921 passed the Emergency Act. Known as the Quota Law, it established limits based on national origin. The number of immigrants from any country would be limited each year to three percent of the number of people from that country living in the United States at the time of the 1910 census.

The new ruling created havoc for thousands caught in midpassage to the United States when at the stroke of midnight, August 1, 1921, the Quota Law went into effect. It started a steamship race. Twenty ships with twenty-five thousand passengers rushed through the Narrows. The first ships to get through quarantine would obtain preference for their passengers under the new law, which affected cabin class as well as steerage.

At anchor in the port of New York were ships filled with anxious, fearful people who did not know whether they would be permitted to land. At any one time vessels flying flags of Italy, Greece, Poland, Sweden, and Germany were moored in the harbor. Rather than return passengers to their native country at steamship company expense, ships preferred to wait around to get in under the next month's quota. In some instances immigrants were detained at Ellis

Island overnight only to be shipped back because the quota was filled.

Still, immigration from eastern and southern Europe continued. To decrease further the flow of people, another law passed Congress. In 1924 the Quota Act all but shut the gates. The new ruling cut to two percent of the 1890 census aliens of a particular national origin to be admitted. It shifted emphasis back to the year when most immigrants had come from northern and western Europe. By 1927 annual immigration from all countries was reduced to one hundred fifty thousand. Ellis Island officials were retrained to regulate aliens under the terms of the quota.

New processing regulations were also put into effect.

These required immigrants to pass examinations and apply for visas at U.S. consulates in their own countries. To assist the consuls, Ellis Island inspectors were sent over as technical advisers.

The shift in regulatory procedures, the cutbacks in immigration, and the Great Depression of the 1930s, reduced arrivals to a trickle—about thirty-five thousand annually.

Ellis Island became a wasteland. No longer, as in Sam Ellis's day, a barren speck of scarcely three acres, here were 27.54 acres of landfill on which had been built a series of mighty stone and brick edifices. The island was not immediately abandoned. During World War II, 1941–45, wounded soldiers were shipped there for rehabilitation; and the Coast Guard used it as a training center. In 1951 it briefly became a playground for children of detained immigrants. But as a Federal Detention Center, it saw unexpected activity in the early 1950s.

In what is now called the Cold War, the country went through another anticommunist crusade. This one was dominated by the figure of Senator Joseph McCarthy, who held a powerful position as head of Senate investigations committees. In hearings that received worldwide coverage, he recklessly accused thousands of being communists and therefore subversives. Despite flimsy evidence, names were recorded on a blacklist, along with so-called communist front organizations. Those accused were often influential men and women in the arts, movies, theater, government, and labor circles.

Among those charged, many opposed the investigations. A few stalwarts went to jail. Others, to protect their jobs and to get their names off the blacklist, publicly confessed to alleged subversive connections; they bowed to McCarthy's pressure and named friends and colleagues as

Communists. It was a time of great fear and feelings of degradation. People were afraid to speak up; jobs were lost, careers smashed, lives ruined, and health shattered. "It was like having a hand at one's throat," said Morris Carnovsky, a blacklisted actor. Among those singled out as a "danger to the country" were alien residents.

In its final days the Registry Hall at Ellis Island resounded to different voices. Not to those arriving, but to those departing. Not to joy, but to anger at baseless accusations.

British journalist Cedric Belfrage was caught in the McCarthy inquisition. He was arrested one day at his desk at the offices of the *National Guardian,* a progressive weekly. On a deportation warrant he was removed to Ellis Island as a "dangerous alien." He said, "We always hear all these beautiful things about Ellis Island about people coming in, you know, 'Give me your tired, your poor. . . .' They don't refer to the last chapter at Ellis Island as a Federal Detention Center involved in throwing people out."

Ellis Island had come to the end of a long road. It had changed shape, size, and purpose, reflecting the country's history. It not only mirrored events; it dealt with people, millions of people, their passions and fears, and their spirit.

In 1954 Ellis Island closed its doors. The weather and vandals took it over. Dark and gloomy, filled with ghosts and shadows, it looked gothic in its ruin. Spectral voices of children bounced off the empty walls. Here and there were broken-down cribs, chests of drawers, lopsided desks, rusted bathrooms, empty benches, bathhouses, and an abandoned chapel. Rubbish was strewn over cracked floors. But the huge crystal and brass fixtures suspended from domed ceilings, the arched windows, wooden balustrades, and massive staircases defied decay.

In 1965 a presidential proclamation declared Ellis Island

a part of the Statue of Liberty National Monument. This act guaranteed its future restoration and care under the National Park Service.

What kind of island will it next become? Some say it will be connected to the mainland of New Jersey by landfill and no longer be an island. Nevertheless, in the 1980s one hundred million Americans (about 40 percent of the population) can trace their ancestry to family members who entered this country through Ellis Island. For them, it will always be an island. When they hand down their history to their children, they will say—*Once there was a tiny island and it grew and grew. It was named for Samuel Ellis, a wholesale dealer in fish, who lived at the time of the American Revolution. In those days it was called Sam Ellis's Island.*

Author's Notes

Most of my research for this book was done at the New-York Historical Society and I would like to express my thanks to the members of the library staff for their cooperation.

Page
4   "Fat shad, Lean shad" in Thomas F. DeVoe, *The Market Book*, p. 313.

9   Henry Hudson's assistant navigator, Robert Juet, kept a journal of the voyage up the Hudson River. See I. N. Stokes, *The Iconography of Manhattan Island*, vol. 1, p. 4.

12   The sale of indentured servants is discussed in Floyd Shumway, *Seaport City; New York in 1775*.

16–17 Historian Martha Lamb quoted in Shumway.

22   William Kelby, head librarian of the New-York Historical Society 1893–98, put together newspaper and magazine articles about early New York City history. His books are very useful: *Notes on Ellis Island; Centennial Notes; The New York Loyalists*, and others.

81

32 Boat found adrift in Kelby, *Manuscript Notes,* p. 21.

35 Federal Hall at 26 Wall Street with its statue of George Washington marks the site of the first inauguration.

42–43 The ballad can be found in S. E. Morison, *Growth of the American Republic,* vol. 2, 1949 ed., p. 184.

51 "A large red wart" in Rodman Gilder, *The Battery,* p. 146.

57 In 1946 Castle Garden was designated a national monument and is now administered by the National Park Service as Castle Clinton National Monument.

59–61 Annie Moore's arrival is described in the newspaper the *World,* January 2, 1892.

66 Mary Zuk is quoted in D. M. Brownstone, *Island of Hope, Island of Tears,* p. 204.

66 In a letter to the *New York Times,* January 14, 1984, the writer recommended that Ellis Island should be forgotten, that "it offered neither welcome nor haven," but subjected people to humiliation.

72 Henry Cabot Lodge in R. Hoffstadter, *The American Republic,* vol. 2, p. 188 and the following pages.

74 "The Great Deportation Delirium" in Kelby, *Notes on Ellis Island.*

78 Actor Morris Carnovsky discussed his experiences at a meeting on "Censorship" at Lincoln Center Library, New York City, August 14, 1984.

78 Cedric Belfrage is quoted in an interview in the *Guardian,* December 14, 1983.

Books for Further Reading

Anderson, Lydia. *Immigration*. New York: Franklin Watts, 1981.
Earle, Alice Morse. *Colonial Days in Old New York*. New York: Charles Scribner's Sons, 1896; reissued by Singing Tree Press, 1968.
Novotny, Ann. *Strangers at the Door*. New York: The Chatham Press Inc., 1971.
Pitkin, Thomas M. *Keepers of the Gate, A History of Ellis Island*. New York: New York University Press, 1975.
Severn, Bill. *The Immigrant Years*. New York: Julian Messner, 1971.
Siegel, Beatrice. *Lillian Wald of Henry Street*. New York: Macmillan & Co., 1983.
Tifft, Wilton. *Ellis Island*. New York: W. W. Norton & Co., 1971.
Tunis, Edwin. *Oars, Sails and Steam*. New York: Crowell & Co., 1952.

Index